DIAG...
CO...
Showin...
gets to the surface
(not drawn to scale)

MINERS' TRANSPORT

WOODEN ROOF SUPPORTS

STEEL ROOF SUPPORTS

CONVEYOR

CONVEYOR

Air regulator door to control ventilation

A Ladybird
Easy-Reading Book
Series 606B

*This carefully planned reference book
describes how our coal was formed and first
mined, the modern methods by which it is
now brought to the surface, and its many
uses and by-products.*

*Even children whose reading experience
is limited will be encouraged by the
full-colour illustrations and relatively simple
text to find out for themselves about this
vital industry, and at the same time
gain extra reading practice.*

'People at Work'
THE
MINER

by I. & J. HAVENHAND

with illustrations
by JOHN BERRY

Publishers: Ladybird Books Ltd . Loughborough
© Ladybird Books Ltd (formerly Wills & Hepworth Ltd) 1965
Printed in England

THE MINER

The coal that we use to-day began as trees and swamps about two-hundred and fifty million years ago. At that time our country was covered by swamps and thick forests. Every year the leaves fell from the trees and some of the trees died. These rotted down and more trees grew in the hot, steamy forests.

As the surface of the earth settled and changed shape, some of these forests became covered with water. The water brought mud and sand which covered the dead trees and leaves.

7214 0069 8

Millions of years went by and the land-surface changed again and rose above the water. New forests grew and when they died, they too, were covered by water, mud and sand. This happened many times.

The layers of mud, sand and dead trees pressed down on each other. The mud and sand changed into layers of rock. Layers of rock are called strata. The dead forests changed into layers of coal. Layers of coal are called seams.

On some pieces of rock we can see the prints of leaves. These are called fossils.

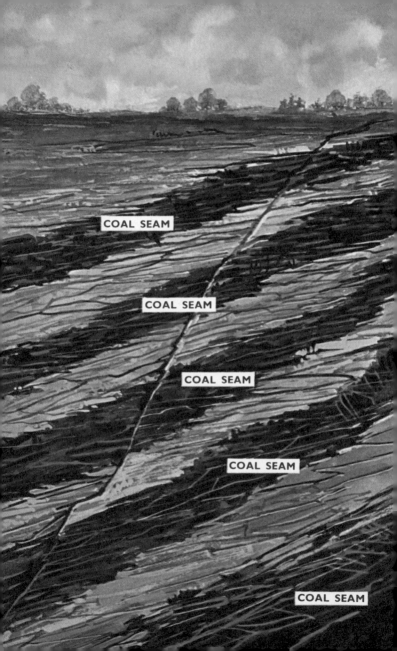

No one knows who discovered that coal would burn. Coal was found in the banks of rivers that had cut into the earth. It was also found on some hillsides where the edges of the seams showed above the ground. This coal is called outcrop coal.

People dug away at the outcrop and started the first coal-mines. When no more coal could be got from the outcrop, the early miners dug pits to reach it.

The early pits were called bell-pits and they were not very deep.

A bell-pit had a narrow shaft or opening, and when coal was found the miner made a large hole. He passed the coal up to the top in baskets pulled up by a rope. When the sides of the hole fell in, the miner left the hole and made another one nearby.

Later, the miners made the pits deeper as they looked for new coal seams. The miners learned how to hold up the roof of the mine by putting in props of timber. They could then work a long way from the pit-shaft.

When the mine workings were further away from the pit-shaft, more people were needed to move the coal. At first, women and young children dragged baskets and trucks of coal through the tunnels under the ground.

Later, ponies were used to pull small trucks, called tubs, on narrow railway lines. The pit-ponies lived in stables at the pit-bottom, and many of them never saw daylight.

To-day the coal is carried in mine cars which are pulled electrically or by diesel engines.

The shafts of early mines were not very deep because deeper mines flooded. Mines were made deeper after steam engines, like the one in the picture, had been invented. Steam engines were used to pump the water out of the mines.

Wire-rope was also invented. With wire-rope and better steam engines, bigger loads could be lifted up and down the mine shafts.

To-day every mine must have two shafts and everything goes up or down these shafts. One is called the upcast and the other is called the downcast.

There is great danger in mines from gas. The gas is called fire-damp and it explodes if a flame gets near it. The early miners had to use candles to be able to work. Sometimes the candles set the gas alight and caused explosions.

To-day, fans near the top of the upcast shaft suck out the used air, and the firedamp, through large funnels (as shown in the picture.) This causes fresh air to be pulled in at the downcast and passed through the mine.

No matches are taken down a mine, and great care is taken not to make sparks.

A lamp which had a flame, but which did not set fire to the gas, was a great help to miners. It was called the Davy Safety Lamp. The miner in the picture is holding one.

The miner also has a lamp fixed to his helmet so that he can see to work. The lamp is lit by a battery which is fixed on the miner's belt.

By counting the lamps that are given out each day, the lamp-man knows how many miners are down the mine.

To-day, the main tunnels in mines are lit by electric lights and some of the coal-faces also now have them.

The miners are taken to and from the pit-bottom in cages. These are like lifts, and each cage has two decks. There are two cages in each shaft and when one cage is at the top the other is at the bottom.

When the top cage is loaded, a man called the banksman signals to the engine-man at the winding house. The engine-man then waits for a signal from the onsetter at the bottom cage. After he has had both signals, the engine-man starts the winding gear.

The cages never carry men and coal together. The banksman and onsetter signal to the winding engine-man what the cages are carrying. When the cages are carrying men, the winding gear is run slower than if coal is being lifted.

At the pit-bottom many tunnels lead off into the mine. The roofs of the tunnels are held up by strong steel girders. Some of the tunnels lead to the coal-face. Others lead to store-rooms, work-shops, loco-garages, the first-aid room and the fire-station.

Narrow railway lines lead to the coal-face. This may be as far as six miles away. If the coal-face is far away the miners ride on rail-cars pulled by diesel locomotives.

Near the coal-face the roof is lower and the miners may have to bend down as they walk. The only lights are those on their helmets.

The coal-face is a shining layer of coal trapped between layers of rock. Near the coal-face are the machines the miners use to cut out the coal.

One machine is called a coal-cutter and works by an electric motor. The coal-cutter has a long cutting arm with steel teeth. The cutting-arm is pushed into a slot at the bottom of the coal-seam. As the cutter moves, it cuts a slot about five feet deep along the coal-face.

After the coal-cutter has moved along, other miners drill deep holes into the coal-face. The holes are for explosive charges which will break down the coal-face.

A miner called a shot-firer tests for gas near the coal-face. If it is safe, the shot-firer puts in the explosives and fills up the holes with clay. Each explosive shot has a wire leading from it. The wires lead to an exploder which is well away from the coal-face.

When all the shots are ready, the miners move away to a safe place. The shot-firer tests again for gas, and then presses a plunger which sets off the explosive shots. The wall of coal breaks away from the seam.

The broken coal at the coal-face has to be moved to the pit-bottom. Miners shovel the coal on to a machine called a conveyor. This is a wide plastic belt which moves along rollers like the tracks on an army tank.

In some mines, machines cut the coal and load it on to conveyors as the cutter moves along the coal-face.

The conveyor carries the coal to the main road that leads to the pit-bottom. The coal is tipped off the conveyor into mine-cars.

Small locomotives pull the loaded mine-cars to the pit-bottom. There the mine-cars are run into the cage or tipped into larger coal carriers called skips. The onsetter signals to the winding engine-man and the coal is quickly taken to the pit-top.

As soon as the coal is cleared from the coal-face, the miners must make the roof safe. Then they move the coal-cutting machine up to the coal-face again. The cutter is made ready to take the next slice of coal from the coal-seam.

At the pit-top, the mine-cars move on to the coal preparation plant. This is a large building standing on stilts with railway tracks underneath it.

The mine-cars are weighed and pass into a machine called a tippler. This tips the coal out on to a conveyor belt. This belt moves the coal under magnets which take out any bits of metal, as you can see in the picture.

The coal has to be sorted into three sizes, very large, medium and small. This is called screening the coal.

The screens are strong metal sheets with different sized holes in them. The small coal is shaken through the small holes, and the medium sized coal is shaken through bigger holes. The very large lumps are tipped off at the end.

The small coal is very dirty and it has to go into the washing-plant. The water takes the dirt and dust away, and leaves the coal clean and ready for use.

When the coal has been sorted and washed, it passes into railway-wagons underneath the coal preparation plant.

There are pit tips near most coal-mines. These tips are made of the dirt and stone that have had to be moved to get out the coal. Some of the dirt is left in the mine, but some has to be taken away.

At the pit-top, the dirt is tipped into large buckets. The buckets move along high wire ropes to the tip.

To-day many tips are levelled off by bulldozers. When the tip is not used, it is covered with soil so that bushes and grass will grow on it.

Even though miners get very dirty at work they do not go home dirty. This is because there are baths at the colliery.

At the pit-head baths every miner has two lockers. When they go to work, the miners put on their working clothes from the dirty locker. After work the miners have a shower-bath and put on their clean clothes from their clean clothes-locker.

There is a canteen near the baths. In the canteen, the miners can buy cups of tea or meals before they go home.

Some coal-seams are not very far under the ground. The coal is dug out by open-cast mining. At open-cast mines there are no shafts.

Very big machines are used to dig away the soil and rock on top of the coal. Some of these machines are like cranes. They are on legs and can even move along as the earth is dug away. The machines scoop up the earth and dump it out of the way. Other digging machines load the coal into lorries which take it away.

Every year about one-hundred and thirty million tons of coal are mined. All this coal has to be moved from the coal-mines to the people who use it. The coal is carried by lorries and by boats and on the railways, to all parts of the country.

Coal is still burned in many homes. Factories and the mines themselves use coal. Power-stations like that in the picture, burn coal to make electricity. Where there are gas-works, coal is used to make gas and coke. Other kinds of works, called coke ovens, use a lot of coal.

At the coke ovens and the gas-works the coal is baked in large ovens. Gas then comes from the coal and coke is left. Most of the coke is sent to iron and steel-works. The rest of the coke is burned as a smokeless fuel in domestic fires and boilers.

Thousands of other important things, as well as coke and gas, are made at the coke ovens. These things are called by-products of coal. They are useful, but do not look as though they started as a piece of coal.

Here are some of the by-products that are made from coal:

Tar for using on roads.

Fertilizers to make plants grow.

Explosives for use in mines, quarries and armaments.

Saccharin for making things sweet, instead of sugar.

Sprays to help farmers to kill weeds and insect pests.

Other things which we see around us that are by-products of coal are *soap* and *washing-powders; aspirin, moth balls, disinfectant* and *perfume; paint, linoleum* and *dyes; plastics, nylon* and *acid.*

ROAD TAR

DRUGS

DETERGENTS

EXPLOSIVES

ANILINE DYES

WEED KILLERS

SACCHARIN

PAINT & VARNISH

NYLON

SULPHURIC ACID

INSECTICIDES

FRUIT TREE SPRAYS

HOUSEHOLD
CLEANSERS

IRON SMELTING

FERTILIZERS

The map at the end of the book shows the most important coalfields in our country.

To-day some of the seams and some of the coalfields are nearly worked out. Teams of men are always seeking new coal-seams or following old ones. This is to make sure that there will always be plenty of coal. The men drill holes deep into the ground where there might be coal.

Coal-seams are sometimes under the sea bed. Special sea boring towers are used to find these seams.

Fife and
Clackmannan

Lothians

Lanarkshire

Ayrshire

Northumberland

Cumbria

Durham

West Yorkshire

South Yorkshire

Nottinghamshire

Lancashire and
Cheshire

North Wales